Write, Read, Listen

Your Handy Writing Coach

by Valerie Haynes Perry

WRITE, READ, LISTEN

YOUR HANDY WRITING COACH

by Valerie HAYNES PERRY

Featuring

Amber Lynn CHILDRESS
Miriam CHING YOON LOUIE
Denise A. COTTON-ROYAL
Danita EASON
Taisa M. GRANT
HADIAH
Lang Kenneth HAYNES
Chelsea LYONS
Marty MATTHEWS
Molly McARDLE
Frederick Douglass PERRY
Paul RICHARDS
Nina SERRANO
Deleign THOMPSON
Deborah WAFER
Tumikia WATU-KHUTHAZA
Yodassa WILLIAMS

ISBN 10: 1548415251

ISBN 13: 978-1548415259

Writing Reference

Second Edition, 2015

Published with LitHive

Also by the author:

Tanner Blue

Music for the Dream—Seven Short Stories

Painted Deserts

Members

Listening Out Loud—A Friend to the Serious Writer

ACKNOWLEDGMENTS

Thank you, Joyce Gordon, for inviting our writing circle to meet in your magnificent art gallery. How fortuitous it was to begin the circles in November of 2014—the year of your tenth anniversary as the creator of the gallery.

Anca Mosiou, thank you for welcoming our writing circle so graciously and enthusiastically to Tech Liminal—your user-friendly coworking space. We're grateful to be part of your community.

Mary Farrell, librarian at the Lakeview branch, thank you so much for welcoming us each year.

Anna Edmondson, Lisa Fuller, Jamie Greenwood, and Elaine Betts—thank you for that transformative weekend in Inverness. Anna, your spectacular vision and intuition brought our community into being. I greatly appreciate your generosity. Everyone: thank you for your insightful input into the first chapter of this book; I've applied your invaluable suggestions.

You all make the world a better place.

TABLE OF CONTENTS

PREFACE

Writing, reading, and listening are all preceded by thinking. If only for a split second, we think about writing before we actually write.

The words that best describe my growth as a writer over the past few years in particular are *experience* and *experimentation*. The experiment began with the completion of my fifth book, *Listening Out Loud—A Friend to the Serious Writer*. It explores five aspects of voice as they pertain to creative writing:

- Voice as sound
- Physical voice
- Stylistic voice
- Voice as discipline
- POV (point of view)

Once the book became available, I facilitated writing circles at several local venues including public libraries. It appeared that there was a gulf between my intentions and the actual results, but that is an inherent part of writing. We write with particular ideas in mind and readers apply their individual interpretations. However, I feel there's still work to be done in clarifying and communicating the five points that I wish to make about how voice informs writing. *Write, Read, Listen* extends that exploration. I believe this book holds at least one idea, solution, or item of importance especially for you. Books come into our lives in all kinds of ways; I'm grateful that this one has found its way to you.

Valerie Haynes Perry

Inverness, California

March 15, 2015

INTRODUCTION

The goal of this book is to help the serious writer recognize and develop their literary voice. How do you know if you're a serious writer? For the purposes of this book, a *serious writer* is simply someone who will do the work of completing a manuscript. This quest entails writing, reading, and listening. *Write, Read, Listen—Your Handy Writing Coach* follows a straightforward structure, dedicating a succinct and plain chapter to each of these topics. Like any other endeavor, a main ingredient for your success is a healthy dose of openness.

"Insights" conclude each chapter to comfort, encourage, and guide you.

Tell your story well.

FIRST Chapter

Writing

My first work in the publishing industry was as a "word processor." That job entailed transferring copyedited manuscripts from paper to a word-processing program. At the time, it was WordPerfect, which was an industry standard before Microsoft Word took the lead. Dedicated machines were also called *word processors*.

As I became comfortable with word processing, my interest in other aspects of publishing grew. I learned how to proofread; lay out text and graphics; edit; and create indexes for books. The sum of these experiences allowed me to freelance and my business name, The Word Process, evolved quite organically.

My previous book, *Listening Out Loud—A Friend to the Serious Writer*, describes the moment when I became a writer. That realization was powered by listening to voice as discipline. *Write, Read, Listen—Your Handy Writing Coach*, unites this necessary trinity of the craft: on some level, all authors must write, read, and listen.

Writing begins with your own, personal point of departure. All you have to do is start, pick up where you left off, or continue. That's it. Fiction, nonfiction—doesn't matter. You don't *have* to finish anything, but completion is its own reward. Writing is your sanctuary—a homecoming that is rent and mortgage free.

There is something very human about Writing as an entity. Stubbornly, it can flood you with thoughts and ideas that insist on being written down. Hard headed, yes, and righteously so because once you join forces with your literary voice, it's always there for you.

We can write about anything. Here's an example. One day, I was in Starbucks Coffee and a large truck drove by. I heard the gears shifting and struggling to make a sharp turn into a parking lot. Behind me, two people were having an intellectual conversation and one person was doing most of the talking. Background musak played. At the same time, I smelled coffee. I saw some bike riders turn into the same parking lot where the large truck made its turn. I felt the smooth touch of the keys on my netbook. The delicate flavors of a nonfat, unsweetened green-tea latte left their taste in my mouth. In order to weave together all of those senses, I listened to their composition. It sounded like this:

> *Danny, the driver of the Safeway truck had just enough energy left to make his Easter-day delivery. His fatigue got the best of him for just one moment, as he snapped his neck away from the café and back toward the busy parking lot. It was Sunday, a day off for everyone else but him, it seemed. Outside of his control, he heard the conversations of all the*

people behind those cool plates of glass in the suburb where he someday hoped to live. He could not help but stare at them, neither with envy, nor resentment—worse yet, he was as neutral as the transmission of his truck when he finally ended its movement. For just a moment, he collapsed back into his seat and rolled down the window all the way to mix some fresh air with the smells of stale fast food, oil, gas, and rubber that were his companions while on the road. The rough and rugged cover on the steering wheel nagged him for replacement at the same time daring him to disregard its loyalty over many, many years. Janine, the new barista, knocked on the passenger door. She handed him a cup of coffee. Their eyes locked, acknowledging the value of a good day's paid work. The driver nodded, "Thank you," and drifted off to caffeine-flavored dreams.

We are constantly surrounded by stories. They are written inside our heads and can stay there unless we liberate them onto a page or screen. Look around right now. What can you write about if you wish to do so?

Clearly, creative writing is entirely voluntary. For some, it's enough to let stories tell themselves through our perceptions, alone. For others, destiny requires that we write down those stories to fulfill a purpose and share with others.

Now, let me venture an assumption: You're reading these words, right here, right now, because destiny is demanding *something* from you that is related to writing.

You're ready to take the next step of concentrating on expression.

Concentrating on Expression

The title of Chapter 5 in Listening Out Loud is "Tricking Writer's Block." The take-home message is we're not obligated to experience writer's block—in fact, we can skip it, altogether. Please keep this fact in mind as we explore the current topic: concentrating on expression.

In meeting writers for the first time, sometimes they'll say something like, "English wasn't my best subject," then, perhaps a little self-consciously, "My grammar's not that good." Fortunately, neither of these is required in order to **express yourself** effectively as a writer. Be kind to yourself and learn to let go of any inhibitions that have prevented you from taking yourself seriously as a writer up until this point. This is a brand-new, brilliant moment in which you can recognize that you have always been free to write. All that remains is your resolve to exercise your **freedom of expression**. Make that leap from resolving to write to producing some written work. Then, you'll be well on your way to discovering your literary voice.

Diving Beneath the Words

Feelings are the undercurrents of words. When we dive beneath the surface of a sentence, paragraph, or page, we experience a transformation from the literal to what we envision based on our individual experience. We have our imaginations to thank for this phenomenon.

Consider this simple statement:

The boy sat down.

Is it possible for your mind to stop the action right there or have you already begun to wonder what happens next? One way to dive beneath the words is to add to them:

The boy sat down. A warm and gentle breeze stirred his thoughts as if they were buttercream icing mixed by hand in a yellow, ceramic bowl.

How sweet, right?

The boy sat down. A warm and gentle breeze stirred his thoughts as if they were buttercream icing mixed by hand in a yellow, ceramic bowl. Soon, the topping turned as bitter as stunted summer fruit.

What *kind* of summer fruit? Apricots? Cherries? Peaches? What was the catalyst that changed the nature of the initial thoughts? As soon as we take the plunge, we enter into a world of infinite possibilities. As we navigate its current, a story speaks its truth.

◉ Insight ◉

Love everything you write.
Strive to make it stronger as you write more, and more, and more.

SECOND Chapter

Reading avidly is a very effective writing teacher. I used to read fiction almost exclusively. Now, I'm usually reading a novel and a nonfiction title, concurrently. The more I read, the more I have in common with other writers. That is, something in what I read almost always resonates with something that I've written.

When I first started writing, it was very instructive to simply look at pages of books in order to learn the structure of dialogue, for example. At a glance, you can see clever ways to identify who's speaking and also learn some basics of punctuation.

As you take yourself seriously as a writer, you might notice that you read differently than before. It might be more difficult to accept everything you read at face value. Your Inner Voice might whisper things like, "If I were writing this, I'd say it differently, meaning *better*." A healthy way to manage that particular response is to respect the work of other writers regardless of quality (which can be subjective), yet improve your own writing based on observations. In order to experience reading as an activity as fully as possible, it's very useful to comfortably analyze what you read.

Analyzing What You Read

Here are some basic questions that I contemplate while reading the work of other writers:

- What attracted me to this book? How did it come into my life?
- Why do I like (or dislike) this book?
- What do I think of the characters?
- What is my response to the author's use of language?
- Am I in this writer's audience as a reader? Why or why not?
- What single point stands out as a result of reading this book?
- What am I learning about writing as a result of reading this book? How is it making me a better writer?

Recently, I read *The Storyteller* by Mario Vargas Llosa. Here are my answers to the questions that I've just posed.

- How did this book come into my life?

  I was roaming around the shelves of the library, starting from the end of the alphabet when I came to Vargas Llosa. The title of the book was irresistible.

- What attracted me to this book?

  The author is Peruvian and I have an M.A. in Spanish. I'm naturally drawn to just about anything that relates to language. After reading several pages,

I loved the settings—Florence, Italy and the Amazon jungle. I've been to the part of Florence that Vargas Llosa describes and revisited that place through the author's vivid descriptions. I haven't been to the Amazon, but that part of the world fascinates me. So, on the one hand, I experienced an immediate intimacy with Florence because I've been there. On the other hand, I was transported to the Amazon through my imagination. It was the best of both worlds for me as a reader—being able to relate personally and rely on the pictures that Vargas Llosa painted in my mind.

+ Why do I like (or dislike) this book?

I like this book very much because it's thought provoking. It's a very nonlinear story and I love Vargas Llosa's sense of abstraction.

+ What do I think of the characters?

The main characters are indigenous people (*Machiguengas*) on one side, and linguists on the other. They all feel believable and they're all well drawn. My favorite character is the *hablador*—the speaker.

+ What is my response to the author's use of language?

Because the linguists are academics, their language is technical, yet it is accessible to the general reader. The language related to the *hablador* feels appropriately mystical.

- Am I in this writer's audience as a reader? Why or why not?

  I'm in Vargas Llosa's audience. I love the variety and originality of his body of work.

- What single point stands out?

  The irony of how the "expert" linguists failed to recognize the importance of the *hablador*.

- What have I learned about writing as a result of reading this book? How has it made me a better writer?

  Vargas Llosa won the 2010 Nobel Prize in Literature. Reading *The Storyteller* reminded me of the importance of responsibly breaking rules once we fully understand their purposes. For example, Vargas Llosa inserts himself into this book in order to make certain political statements. This form of *editorializing* is sometimes discouraged because it can be perceived as interrupting the flow of a story and rupturing the narrative voice. However, Vargas Llosa uses his artistic license in meaningful ways that serve his stories well. His work encourages me to continue to trust my ongoing growth as a serious writer.

What are you reading?

Take the next few pages to answer these questions for yourself. Think about the questions carefully—not too much, not too little—just enough. Use your answers to move forward with your own story as a serious writer.

What attracted you to this book? How did it come into your life?

Why do you like (or dislike) this book?

What do you think of the characters?

What is your response to the author's use of language?

Are you in this writer's audience as a reader? Why or why not?

What single point stands out?

What are you learning about writing as a result of reading this book? How is it making you a better writer?

Four Valuable Autographs

This section lists four books I've read that contain inscriptions from the authors. Each writer has an impressive body of work. Interacting with published authors can be a tremendous source of inspiration. If you buy books from them at their readings; get the books signed; and tell them you're a writer, yourself, there's a good chance that the writers will encourage you in some way. It can make you feel "like one of them" as you work on authoring books of your own.

Here's what four authors wrote in my copies of their books:

Paule Marshall: *Brown Girl, Brownstones*

"Stay strong, write well."

Caryl Phillips: *Dancing in the Dark*

"Good luck in your own writing. Don't give up!"

Zadie Smith, *White Teeth*

"Keep writing etc (but remember to bathe, eat)."

Alfredo Vea, *Gods Go Begging*

"Keep on writing."

I asked Ms. Marshall about graceful ways to change points of view within the same story. She said, "Do what makes sense." Following this advice has helped me trust my instincts and skills as a writer. It always comes down to doing what best serves the storytelling. In other words, "Tell your story well." I hope the clear pattern in all of this advice is useful to you.

☉ Insight ☉

Carefully choose the books you read and cultivate reading as a habit.
Use reading to improve your skills as a writer.

THIRD Chapter

Listening

Listening requires some measure of stillness and silence in the mind. Those qualities can responsibly transform hearing into deep listening and meaningful written work. Often, we process what we hear automatically before a speaker has finished talking. No wonder it's so easy for one person to misunderstand another.

Many function from a place of incomplete receipt of information. Fortunately, awareness comes to the rescue in a variety of situations. That is the case with developing the skill of **listening**, which is invaluable to our growth as writers. We engage analytical skills as we read words or listen to them being spoken. As a result, the phenomenon of "reading between the lines" emerges, which fundamentally, involves deep listening.

Learning to Listen

In a writing circle, a very particular type of intuition forms as the result of listening deeply. This intuition allows each writer to fill in blanks that arise at the subjective level. Some writers refer to these "blanks" as writer's block.

Trusting this intuition and allowing for a necessary pause are the basic requirements for dissolving such blocks. This type of "literary listening" is a selfless act that rewards all of its serious practitioners with a story that is told well.

How do you learn to listen as a writer? Here are some things to listen *for* when participating in a writing circle or at a public reading:

- How or what you feel when someone else reads

  Are you engaged? Is the reader confident and engaged?

- The tone and pacing of the reader's voice

  Are they appropriate for the content of the story? Are transitions between narrative and dialogue expressed clearly?

- Credibility of the characters

  Do you feel like you know the characters and their motivations? Do you like, dislike, admire, or care about them? Do you associate any other emotions with the characters?

- Specific descriptions that spark images

  Can you always see what you're hearing?

- Messages of any type

  Do you have a clear sense of the key points of the story?

- Exceptional passages

  Do you consider any specific sentences particularly well crafted?

- Areas that would benefit from revision

  Does the quality of the writing ever seem unclear or disconnected?

There's a good chance that you're posing all of these questions naturally as you listen to readings. Maybe all you need to do is heighten your awareness of these elements in order to boost your present skill level.

Keep in mind that the purpose of sharpening your listening skills is to improve your personal technique and also to enjoy the work of fellow writers more fully.

Now that you've learned to listen more deeply to your fellow writers as they read their work, consider the importance and benefits of reading aloud.

Reading Aloud

As a writing coach, I emphasize the importance of reading aloud. Doing so enhances the process of discovering and consistently recognizing your literary voice. We hear words in one way inside our heads and in another when our physical voices set the words free. Something gets *changed* in this translation. Yet, there is a language of the mind that corresponds to our power of speech.

Writers are often taken aback by how their words sound when vocalized. Here are some of the benefits of reading aloud:

- Facilitating the editorial process

    When a passage doesn't feel or sound right when read, it calls for editing.

- Building confidence

    Writers who are initially shy about reading aloud often become comfortable with this activity before too long. Reading aloud becomes a very natural extension of the writing process.

- Entertaining

    It's fun for writers and listeners to get into the drama of reading aloud.

- Testing engagement

    This goes for the writer as well as listeners. It's also related to "Facilitating the editorial process" at the beginning of this list. Lack of engagement is a sign that revision is called for.

These are just a few examples of how reading aloud can be useful. You can add to this list on any of the Room to Write pages at the end of this book.

⊙ Insight ⊙

We're inspired by all kinds of stimuli. In order to translate those effects into a language that our readers can understand, we must listen deeply for the best ways to tell our stories. Reading aloud enhances the interactive experience that exists between writers and their listeners.

APPENDIX A

Prompts

Now, it's time for you to do some writing of your own
Here are nine prompts to help you get started.

Prompt #1: Back to the Womb

Prompt #4: Migration

Prompt #5: Infinity

Prompt #6: The Blinking Eye

Prompt #7: Food Is Something to Do

Prompt #8: Life's Best

Prompt #9: Doggie Diplomats

APPENDIX B

Author's Writing from Prompts

At the beginning of circles, I often ask participants to write about something that stands out in their minds from a point earlier in that day. Prompts are often products of simple observations. The writing that they inspire can be abstract, linear, profound, and it is usually surprising.

We can write *anything*, which is exactly what I've done here in response to the prompts in Appendix A. These samples are lightly edited. A character from my first novel, *Tanner Blue*, makes a few cameo appearances. Her name is Jiaré.

Prompt #1: Back to the Womb

Comfort-warmth

umbilical and haven forming.

Dive up to the birth canal.

Stillness is a single rhythm.

Warm waters of the womb.

Prompt #2: Microwaves Make Good Clocks

Both Paulo Coelho and Dr. Neil DeGrasse Tyson have pointed out that time is an illusion. Change is real, measured in millennia, years, and by evidence of evolution, yet there is no law demanding its dependence upon hours, months, or dates. Through it all, microwaves do, indeed, make good clocks once you master how to enter certain numbers.

Prompt #3: Outer Space

Turns out there is more than one universe, making it a multiverse, meaning that experiences can be multiversal, traveling beyond galaxies and solar systems, planets, shooting stars, and moons; comets chasing their own tails, running around in outer space.

Prompt #4: Migration

The news reader's voice was full of instigation. According to him, "illegals" oozed from Mexico into the States of America across a fabricated line. The longer Jiaré listened, the more the droning voice became a score for the migratory practices of birds. Year round, they flew from one place to another circling the earth.

Flight can be a legal song that guides the paths of nomads.

Prompt #5: Infinity

Does infinity apply to everything? Shapes can be traced over and over again, forever. Words can be repeated by accident or on purpose. A car can drive in circles, squares, and sharpened triangles only to find that the shortest distance follows one straight line.

Prompt #6: The Blinking Eye

One two, three, four, walking on the miniature stair-stepper in front of a bedroom window, Jiaré notices a small hole in the mauve, wood fence that delineates where her backyard ends and the neighbor's starts. Up down, down up, her vertical movement brings into view a thin strip of molding perceived through the little aperture in the fence. The strip becomes an eyeball bobbing up and down within an upper and a lower lid as her feet depress and release the pneumatic mechanism on the plastic exercise machine. She listens to jazz, says prayers, and meditates in the course of 30 minutes to the blinking eye that is her private metronome.

Prompt #7: Food Is Something to Do

"Are you hungry?"

"*Hungry?*"

"You know, is your stomach growling or maybe it feels empty?"

"No. I just want to eat. Gives me something to do."

"Want to walk or something until you're hungry?"

"No. I have a taste for some South American food. We live in a place where we can have anything. Hey, what about you—are you hungry?"

"Yeah, but I want to wait a while to eat."

"What for?"

"I've got some other things to do."

Prompt #8: Life's Best

The wooden crate was upside down in the city's sector known as 'Chinatown.' The driver pulled into a space as another car left the vacancy behind. He sat there for the longest time wanting to get out and turn the box so its message would be easier to read. Red circles were painted on the crate—maybe apples or plums despite the fact the contents were knotted lengths of ginger. As noon turned to dusk the man reflected on his past. He started his car and eased away from the curb, praying that the words on the crate described his future.

Prompt #9: Doggie Diplomats

Dogs will have their own cars and customized license plates like all the other diplomats, one day. More and more, dogless people are being ignored and talked about, but not addressed, directly.

Is it a mix? How old is she? Oh, it's a 'he;' I should have looked closer. Oh, it's purebred. Does he have papers? Are you taking him to shows—not to see them, to be in them? What kind of food does he eat? No table scraps—of course not. Top of the line. Right. Thanks for talking to me.

My bike's in the shop. I can't afford to take a bus. If I start walking now, I can get back to the shelter before it's full.

Appendix C

The Speaking Circle

I've breathed the same air while writing with almost all of the following writers. I'm grateful that they all said, "Yes," when I asked them to contribute to this book. All of the following work was written spontaneously, either from writing prompts within the circle or by other purely organic means. It is a particular pleasure and privilege for me to hear their physical voices read me their stories as I revisit their words on the pages of this book.

Musical Chairs

Amber Lynn CHILDRESS

We are all standing in a circle surrounded by chairs. All of us but one, the one who seems to be in charge. I am in a state of confusion, these people are all strangers to me, yet many of them look like folks I know. There is a woman who resembles my mother. Another resembles my sister, another, my dad and there is even one who resembles my best friend! I feel my heart racing; it's about to jump out of my chest. What in the hell is going on? It seems like I am staring at all of these people for hours; yet only a few seconds pass. Then the music begins. It reminds me of a carousel—my head is spinning like one. Everyone begins to walk around the circle of chairs, so I follow suit. The music stops and everyone scrambles to a chair, like their life depends on it. I grab a seat, not sure what the penalty is for the one left standing. The woman who resembles my mother is left chairless. She spots me. I look down. My facial expression and body movement are like that of an unprepared student trying to avoid the teacher. The woman walks towards me. I look around, all eyes are glued on me. The woman looks sad, her eyes plead with me. I don't know this woman. I don't know the punishment. I don't want to get up. She stares, pleading with me. I don't want to get up. My feet are not obeying me. Why is this happening? I slowly stand up out of my chair. People are beginning to whisper. What is going on?

ode to dust

Miriam CHING YOON LOUIE

for minnie, born in reedley, "world's fruit basket"

throw your arms wide, mama, spin
under almond tree envying your eyes
eleventh & last child of migrant parents
because they plant new soil each season you
will live in future of where they were last seen

rooster shouts to dawn: *wake up!* you rise
thru blanket great plains topsoil flew in
fresh last night heralding battalions hungry
jalopies your okie arkie texie mexie friends will
teach you to relish chicken fried steak & bacon fat

gravy how to outrun dirtdevils—or outlast
their whippings how to twirl like dandelion
umbrellas how to parachute from moving cars
you are tornado gathering on my horizon, mama
hug your chest to accelerate speed of your joy

time orchid space

Shade of The Righteous Tree

Denise A. COTTON-ROYAL

From the bowels of our history...

Retribution, restitution,

Onward toward revolution.

Thick, black, hair; juicy lips,

Calloused hands and widened hips.

Glorious eyes sacrifice,

For all have paid a price.

Hallelujah, hallelujah...we sing.

Together we stand, in unity

Under the shade of the righteous tree.

Solidarity shall bring power to the people

To emerge in victory and sing:

Hallelujah, hallelujah...we sing.

Schizomaybe

Danita EASON

You see dirt man circling bags of shit and flies
Singing insanity and fling piss whip like a majorette
swinging a baton
Wearing dirt suit, slime stupor and alleged bad choices
manifested.
Could be crack, could be karma.
Lady tell your kids not to look his way or they'll turn to
stone
Or he'll probably eat them with
monster teeth designed like broken piano keys
Vacant eyes wide as saucers

If one really paid attention, they'd see
But-a-man dressed in courage most envy
As they hold onto their dreams of freedom 'til the only
Escape is their demise
He dances to his own private jam
In the middle of traffic, eyes shut to people laughing at him
He is the center of his galaxy, entertaining gods and
constellations
Escaping a reality that has him homeless, dirty, hungry,
alone, and damaged.

Everyone else is crazy,
Rushing to unfulfilled lives,
Ignoring the voices in their heads that tell them they are
special

That tell them to dance, laugh, play like happy-go-lucky
children
Chained instead to a life that keeps them sedentary and far
from their core.

Freedom is the lens that he sees through.
Settled into him like the staunch of rotting shoes.
No pill could take this away from him.

You see dirt man circling bags of shit and flies
Singing insanity and fling piss whip like a majorette
swinging a baton
Blissfully happy.
He is the envy of all who wish they had the courage

To be his kind of crazy.

They Look Like People

Taisa M. GRANT

They look like people but they don't move quite the same way. They don't actually walk. Most of them sort of glide as they move about. They have two eyes, two arms, two legs and different shades of skin, like most people I know. But when I look closely, I see that they glow. Especially, when they smile. It also appears as if they don't talk like people do. I mean, I just saw a group of them standing in a circle, flailing their arms, hunching over and grabbing their stomachs as anyone would do, while trying to control an uncontrollable laugh. The thing that shook me up though, was there was no sound. Not a loud laugh, a hollering voice. Nothing. There were just smiles and body language. But they are familiar; they look like me and my moms and other friends and family. Then I see her, a beautiful black sistah, at least she looks like one. However, she is flying from the sky, landing into the group but still hovering above the ground, like the rest. This is peculiar to me, I think, *Where the heck am I?* I must be dreaming, I scream the words, "Wake up!" At that point, the silence is broken, the group turns and looks at me. And without saying a word, I hear them in my head. "Can you keep it down? We don't talk that way up here."

HADIAH

I have been breathing to the rhythm of the universe for some time. This practice began at age seven or eight when I ordered a set of small books about our solar system—our universe. I asked my stepfather for a dime or a quarter, which I wrapped up in toilet paper, placed in an envelope, and sent on its way. I was very excited when the books started coming to my house. Some of the pictures were in color and the others, of course, in black and white. They were amazing! I couldn't read all the words though I tried very hard. The pictures blew me toward the heavens, especially, at night. I wanted to work with the people who took those pictures. My friends in the projects messed with me because I spent a lot of time looking up at the sky; their teasing was actually fun. I was always able to teach them something about the night sky and get some of them to join me in looking up at the universe. I became a school teacher instead of an astronomer. My classrooms have a photo of "The Eye of God," which I named after discovering it at the Chabot Space & Science Center, here, in Oakland.

At night, when my heart beats fast and the stress of the day has me in a whirlwind, I calm down and fall asleep by repeating, "My heart beats to the rhythm of the Universe," over and over.

Skipping Stones

Lang Kenneth HAYNES

I

There is a myth about the flatness of skipping stones. It doesn't really matter. What matters are the implications of skipping things, trying to get back to where rocks enter water, tight rings and people working back to that point.

II

Think of the man carrying a full cup of oil through a marketplace without spilling a drop because his concentration was so intense. There's meditation in caves and there's maintaining consciousness no matter what's going on out in the world. Trying to get back, like concentric circles, easy to envision, gradually bigger then less intense. The last circle seen or detected is what people glom onto. This is it, this is where to be. The place where there's a preponderance of people saying this is what we say, think, and feel. It resonates.

III

What sets a great person apart, this is the circle that we want to enter upon. John Winston knows how to fish beyond the last ring. That's where I fish, where I glom onto. The bobber goes down. That's where most say this is the place to be. John says, "You gonna find the fish. Not doing the usual things." Knowledge outside the rings makes him a great fisherman.

Straight lines

Chelsea LYONS

I am left handed.

Everything I do turns out crooked or off in some way.

I have to turn my paper sideways in order to draw a straight line, and not to mention the tedious process of parting my hair down the middle. (Imagine being on a movie set and the director saying, "Take eleven!")

Society makes me feel backwards. In order to use scissors, I must flip them in the opposite direction. When writing a sentence with an ink pen, my hands smear the words. Even using certain utensils makes me feel uncoordinated. There's no denying it, left-handers are the odd men out, living in a right-handed world.

Only a small majority of us are in our "right" mind.

Hike to Seven Lakes Basin

Marty MATTHEWS

It's cold at this time of the morning, even though it's the middle of August. Even so, I start early so I can get one of the few good campsites. The trail starts off with a gentle climb, lulling me into thinking that it won't be too bad. Less than an hour into the four-hour hike, though, I'm breathing pretty hard, wishing that I packed lighter. There are all sorts of things in my pack that I don't really need, considering I have to carry them up 3,000 feet. After three hours, I'm seriously tired. My legs hurt, my back is killing me, and my pack feels like a huge boulder roughly strapped to my back. At this point, all I can do is put one foot in front of the other. Finally, when I'm certain that I can't go another step, I come out on a high ridge—the High Divide—and look down at the Seven Lakes Basin. Suddenly, the hard climb is all worthwhile. Below, more than seven small lakes are surrounded by alpine meadows lush with wildflowers and blueberries. I can't wait to go down and sit by a lake, bask in the sun, and consider eating some blueberries—like the little brown bear across the lake. Also, that bottle of wine I carried up may not have been such a bad idea after all.

This is one of my favorite places in the world.

++++++++++++++++

Oh.

AHAHAHAHAHAHAHAHA!!!...

I'm sorry, I just didn't see that one coming. No, no, keep typing.

See, it started just the normal way, you know? We all lived our lives, I lived mine... Sure we were good and bad, but ya know, no more than the usual. Even when everything really started? Perfectly innocent as can be, just kids who knew no more than images and descriptions of nothing... Just thinking, or trying at least, dreaming up fantasies of swimming in warm oceans that touched the sky. It was later, not when the blood in our veins began to sing with what one might call love, not even when we spilled it all and then fell to pieces. It was after that, hidden in the beginning by trying to prop each other up and hide the fact that we just wanted to run both to and from each other in our pain... We could only see it when the hot tears dried away and the music stopped. No, the time we became sinners was when we had put our broken ceramic emotions together again, when friends forged by fire and steel no longer needed each other. It was then we could see what we had done. Once seen, it was maliceful, and it was cruel.

In those days, the strongest bonds became just the same act, over and over, and it was the monotony that made steel hearts change and drift away without knowing.

I didn't answer your question, did I? So... one day I saw my footprints on real and false shores, and it ached to see all the damage. So I took us into the icy water of the river's new year, and though not the same, in my dying moment, perhaps then we finally touched that warm sky.

Again Imagine

Frederick Douglass PERRY

Again Imagine

There is a connection
between us
at the DNA level
So tight
Sometimes
it is hard to breathe
In this battlefield
Crushing in on us
No longer a battlefield of ideas
Littered with those
Stacked on the horizon
who no longer hold
their ideals
because they exhausted them
wrapping them in flags

Again Imagine

How could I forget
This honest man
his eyes have held on
all of these years
pointing the way
from strife and drama
To peacefulness
Insha'Allah
have faith

Again Imagine

I am the king of the world
we shout that down from the stage
but this is the kingdom of love
this is the space
where we pray for PEACE

Again Imagine

Imagine what the world would
be like
if each one
could tell their story
raise their song
look into our hearts
and help us
pray for PEACE

Walking the Lake

Paul RICHARDS

Started when I was a kid, maybe 9 years old. Only I rode my bike from home in east Oakland around the lake on the way to the YMCA over on Telegraph Ave during summer to go swimming in their basement pool. It was an adventure at that age. Then one day, right in front of the Kaiser building, I decided to veer left up 20th at the very moment that a PG&E truck, following the Lakeside drive to the right, hit me. Bam! I was chewing gum as I flew through the air, landing on the grass along with my bike. I looked at my bike. The handle bars faced one way, the front tire another. I thought, oh no, Mom is going to take my bike away. So I got up, still chewing that gum, aligned my handle bars as best I could with the tire between my knees and rode off to the sound of the stricken driver asking me if I was ok. And then I spit the gum out. Never told anyone about it until I was driving cars much later. I walked and ran around the lake after that for many years and always replayed that gum chewing incident whenever I came to that spot on the Lake right in front of the Kaiser building.

Gift of the Magi

Nina SERRANO

The weak winter sun began fading and darkening clouds loomed as she entered the shop. Bright Xmas tree lights glowed from the small decorated tree in the window The new 1946 calendars all held a promise of the days to come. She could hardly imagine it.

The war had been over since summer. And it seemed like the whole world was excited not knowing what would happen next, though she knew it would be wonderful. How could it not? We won the war! The Nazi's and Japanese lost. Now the whole world would be free and equal. Dad and many soldiers were already home. Mama was helping her knit him a scarf.

What a joy! She had a pocket of full of money for buying presents. Glancing again through the plate glass she noticed the sky diming faster. Her mother and her little brother Johnny were next door in the grocery. She had promised Mama to be right out and join them. These were her precious moments to pick out their presents without anyone seeing.

Johnny's present was easy. She looked over at the brightly displayed toys: toy soldiers, toy guns, bow and arrow sets, Indian feathered head bands, cowboy hats, rubber knives and marbles. The puzzles were too expensive. She had counted out everything in her piggy back. The coins were weighing down her pocket.

She handed the red handled rubber knife to the sales lady knowing Johnny would be so happy. She raced to the counter with ladies things, mirrors, combs, hair pins, perfumes, and lipsticks. Yes, lipstick for Mama, shiny and bright for her smiles. Mama would love it and best of all, she would love Rosie for choosing it.

Quiet Mind

Deleign THOMPSON

Quiet mind. Ssshhhh. Now let Quiet take us to a rare place, a place we don't know.

Stop. Look around the place we're in. Turn it off. Put it down. Sit down and be still.

Ssshhh mind to our mind. Quietly.

This is very strange to us. Wow! It's beyond our understanding. We don't know this place.

What is *Quiet*? Or *who is* Quiet? Now is Quiet. Why is Quiet looking at us like that?

Now is the time to be Quiet. This is that place, the place that is so rare.

We hear you Quiet.

Ssshhh.

Cougars and the Young President

Deborah WAFER

We were so happy to campaign for, raise money for, vote for, go to the inauguration of Barack Obama. It was all so surreal, so beautiful. The girls, Michelle. We had such expectations, not fully realizing that the work was just beginning. We were not prepared for the Republican/white backlash and later Democratic distancing from the president (and they lost). More important, the treatment of the president was shocking and reminded us that racism is alive and well in this US of A. Worse, every little presidential insult reopened a wound in the wounded.

Some will say he knew what he was getting into. Did he?

Some will say we are taking political insults too personal. Is that true?

Let's talk and listen for positive change we can believe in.

Moth Travels

Tumikia WATU-KHUTHAZA

It got me pondering on BART as I made my trip home this first spring evening. I didn't see it get on the train. I only saw a small brown flash out of the corner of my eye. Searching, I spotted the small brown moth as it frantically fluttered around the train compartment trying desperately to escape.

Briefly, I glanced at nearby passengers to see if they, too, noticed the anxious little moth.

Alas, no one shares my care, lost are they in their intimate conversations. Too involved are they in their musings or mobile devices to notice a small distressed insect.

I watched it find a perch and place to rest. Then lost it when we arrived at the next station as the doors opened allowing passengers to go to and fro. After the doors closed and the new passengers settled, I found it, again. I tried to follow the little moth with my eyes as it quickly fluttered around the compartment smashing into the wall of windows and doors.

From station to station, it continued the pattern of rest and flutter. Until finally, at the North Berkeley station, the moth left its perch, fluttered about, then quickly found its way through the open doors before they closed once again.

A sigh escaped me and I felt myself relax a little at the idea of the little moth's quick escape to freedom.

Thus began my pondering. What, I wondered, does the moth do so far from where it entered the train—possibly so far from home? Suddenly, I realized that I wasn't sure how long it was on the train before I became aware of it after leaving the MacArthur station. Possibly, it could have been on the train much longer than I initially thought. Either way, I knew it was miles away from where it got on the train.

Unlike us, I figured it didn't stop and look at the signs to see where it landed. I wondered if the moth would make a new home at or near the North Berkeley station. Would the little brown moth begin a long journey home? How long would it take? Could a small moth even make such a journey? How long do moths live?

Now it's gone and my journey nears its end. My mind turns to other things.

The Twin Goddesses, Book 1: Revelations (excerpt)

Yodassa WILLIAMS

Inspired by the prompt, "They Look Like People"

I open my eyes to darkness and feel the heavy presence of others; their hot breath in the air, the shuffling of limbs and rustling of clothing.

"Who's there?" I cry into the room. I hear a snicker, a "Shhh" and finally, "Turn on the light, Natalie, she's scared." A nightlight comes on and after a moment I can see around me. I'm in a room with rows of bunk beds and staring at me from them are dozens of young girls. Or at least they were once young girls. They look like people, but not normal ones and not in any condition you've ever heard about. Their faces are gaunt beyond measure, only their pale eyes and teeth are clearly visible. Their entire bodies are sunken and nearly transparent. I think it's a trick of the light, but then a girl turns to the side and I realize I am literally looking through her head.

"Who are you?" I ask them. Another snicker.

"We're imposters, posing as human beings," a voice says from the crowd.

"What do you mean?" I ask, still in the corner and too terrified to move.

"You'll find out soon enough. Vincent will come for you. They never let the fresh meat sit for too long."

Appendix D

Room to Write

These pages are all yours—create your own prompts; preserve ideas until you can write about them; or work on them right now! As a matter of fact, why not put the rest of this page to good use?

Room to Write

Room to Write

Room to Write

Room to Write

Room to Write

Room to Write

Room to Write

Room to Write

Room to Write

Room to Write

Room to Write

Room to Write

Room to Write